OVERCOMING MY SOCIAL PHOBIA

Elena García

CONTENTS

PREFACE

Let me introduce myself. I'm... actually, scratch that. I always try to fly under the radar anyway. But here's something that pretty much sums me up: I don't like people. Okay, it's not like I hate anyone, and I definitely don't wish anyone ill. I'm actually deeply affected by the news, wars, and tragic events. But out there, people are only talked about in the abstract. When the details come up, they feel so distant that they don't even seem real to me.

If I can avoid it—and trust me, I'm an expert at dodging these things—I don't do social events. If I have two routes to choose from, I take the one with less traffic. I only go shopping when the stores are totally empty. I can count my true friendships and loves on one hand. Even saying a simple hello feels like a chore. I'd much rather read, play video games, or watch a movie by myself than hang out with anyone. I don't even like eating out unless I can grab a seat where nobody can see me. I prefer driving over taking the bus, a secluded beach over a crowded one, and...

But I'd better stop there, because you get me. You see yourself in this, and that's exactly why I don't need to explain to you what social phobia is all about.

HOW MY SOCIAL PHOBIA BEGAN

I don't really remember when I became such a grump, because I wasn't always like this. I used to be a "normal" girl—and I put that in quotation marks because I'm not sure if anyone is actually completely normal. But hey, we're the crazy ones who hide, the introverts, the antisocial ones, the loners. We're just not cool. By the way, you'd be surprised to learn that those cool extroverts are often hiding way worse traumas than we are. But maybe they suffer less than we do.

And why do we suffer the most? Some of us suffer because we're forced to socialize at school, work, with family, or around the neighborhood. Others suffer because they have zero life outside their four walls. You can even suffer twice as much, because it's totally possible to be stuck around people when you don't feel like it, while simultaneously missing out on things you actually want to do but can't, simply because everything seems to be designed to be done in a group.

I remember being pretty outgoing and talkative as a kid. But then I went to a strict Catholic school, and back home, someone else was dealing with social anxiety—and oh my gosh, I must have picked up every single one of their habits. I think it happened so gradually that before I knew it, I was just an introverted nerd hitting puberty.

During that incredibly awkward transitional phase, I felt lonely. Deeply lonely. I needed people. After all, we all need people, even if it's just to put food on the table and keep things running. But you know what I mean. I needed companionship, understanding, and connection. I felt like my taste in music, the way I dressed, and my ideas were completely out of sync with my school environment. I had pen pals overseas that I'd talk about music with, and every time I read the sign-off at the end of those letters, "Your friend...", I felt a little bit of comfort.

But before that, I had gone through a severe depression that kept me bedridden for months. I was literally sick from loneliness, and to top it off, I had a hormonal imbalance. Once I got that under control, I felt so much better physically and emotionally. That's when I thought, *"I don't need anyone. I can handle things on my own."* So, I withdrew even further into my shell, and this time, I was happy about it. No one had been there for me when I needed it most, so now that I felt like I didn't need anyone, everyone else could just go to hell.

CHARACTERISTICS OF PEOPLE WHO SUFFER FROM SOCIAL PHOBIA

I have always been smart —"too smart." I've yet to meet a single person with social phobia who isn't. We overthink all the time. When I was ten years old, just thinking about the mysteries of the universe would give me anxiety. And overthinking is never a good thing when you have a tool in your hands that you don't know how to use right. I mean, your own thoughts can make you sick or drive you crazy, or, on the flip side, they can heal you. There's toxic thinking, and then there's healing thinking.

But before I get into that, let me finish my story. I never saw a therapist. My parents never acknowledged my problem, and honestly, they probably would've had to drag me there kicking and screaming. As for other people I know who went to therapy, things didn't turn out all that well for them. In most cases, they just ended up hooked on antidepressants, and that was that.

High school was hell. I got straight A's, but I wasn't happy. Obviously, the two don't always go hand in hand. But in a way, I found comfort in my own little refuge: studying. And that was the exact excuse I used every time someone asked me to go out. Hanging out with strangers? Flirting with guys who only wanted to get laid? How awful! The funny thing is, I loved to dance —but only by myself in my room with the radio blasting.

I was pretty, so it was impossible to fly under the radar. If you're a guy or a girl who struggles with how you look, you might find it hard to believe that someone pretty and smart could deal with social phobia. But the thing is, the problem isn't how we actually look, it's how we feel and how we see ourselves. I was incredibly shy, so getting attention from guys just made things worse. I kissed a guy for the first time when I was 18, and my whole body was shaking. I felt so uncomfortable that I didn't do it again until two decades later.

In the meantime, I buried myself in my career and stayed in higher education until I was in my 30s. At that point, I didn't have to socialize as much. As for parties, I only went to two during that entire time, and both were a massive struggle. If I could skip a lecture and just get the notes, I did. And team meetings? Those completely drained my mental battery.

MY PROBLEM WAS GETTING WORSE

I had been in college for several years and spent most of my summer breaks at home with my parents when I completely collapsed on my first day of class. We had to introduce ourselves to the other students, and I just ran out through the first door I saw. I went home and lay on my bed crying. I kept telling myself, "I'm dead, God, I'm dead inside!" I even changed classes because the professor put way too much emphasis on student participation. Some people actually drop out of school entirely in situations like that, and looking back, that's where I showed my strength.

But I was suffering from severe depression, and the absolute rock bottom came when I was 25. That summer, I woke up crying every single morning, even when I spent a few quiet days with my family at the beach. My only friend at the time was my brother, and I knew he would leave me behind as soon as he got a girlfriend — and that's exactly what happened.

I had a few acquaintances in college —just enough to get by in certain classes— but the few friends I'd made during my first year had already drifted away. Or rather, I had pushed them away because I never felt like going out after class. I hadn't taken those first steps at the right time. At 15, I couldn't push past my shyness to go to bars, and later on, it became flat-out impossible. I was still a complete amateur in areas where everyone else was already a veteran.

They say being young is a blessing, but for me, it was just pure bleakness. I wasted an entire decade doing nothing but the bare minimum, and once I graduated, things got even worse. That's when I truly hit rock bottom.

I kept a notebook where I tracked the days I actually left the house. There were two days a month at most, and even then, it was just to run a quick errand around the corner. I was still living with my parents, and since finding a job wasn't easy, I had the perfect excuse not to move out. The only friend I had left at the time was completely buried in her exams, so our usual walks together stopped. Aside from being hyper-focused on her studies, she was fed up with my aversion to crowded places and my total lack of interest in dating. My past romantic relationships had been purely platonic, and I still preferred to keep myself entertained with books and movies all on my own.

Those months of isolation were devastating for my mental health. I felt completely detached from reality —I guess that's what losing your mind must feel like. I felt miserable all the time. I felt like no one could help me, and I didn't tell a soul how I was feeling. I've always had a phobia of doctors, so seeking professional help wasn't even on the table.

Summer came, and I went on vacation with my parents for a few days, as usual. We were in a quiet, secluded place, and I withdrew even further into myself —even though I didn't think it was humanly possible for me to get any more introverted. I had always lived my life half-heartedly; however, I felt like I had no choice but to keep up appearances so I wouldn't disappoint anyone and could live up to the high standards of perfectionism expected of me at home.

But we were on vacation, and the pressure eased up. When you have unlimited time to overthink, you start to see reality completely unvarnished. And then came my 'dark night of the soul', as I call it. It was the hardest moment of my life so far, but at the same time the best, because I had truly hit rock bottom. And when you're at rock bottom, there's only one thing left to do: climb back up.

EMERGING FROM
ROCK BOTTOM

I must admit that I have never contemplated suicide. I know those cases exist, and maybe you're going through that yourself. But deep down, I actually enjoyed being alone, so the suffering only came when the situation started to overwhelm me. That night, I suffered like never before, feeling an infinite burden. I thought about death, yes, but not because I wanted to cross over to the other side. I just thought about what that moment would be like when everything was finally over... And then, bingo! I found my healing thought: "Someday, everything will be over."

It's hard to put into words what I felt. It was like realizing how foolish it is to suffer unnecessarily in this life. No matter what you do or what happens, there is always an end waiting for us. We don't know what comes next, but one thing is for sure: we're all going to die someday. So what nonsense it is to suffer over nothing. The truth is, death puts everything into perspective.

Our lives are deeply connected to our deaths. Philosophers have theorized about this for centuries, and how we view death completely shapes how we experience life. Those who fear God live their lives trying to avoid sin so they won't be punished in the afterlife. On the other hand, those who believe in nothing throw themselves into enjoying life as much as humanly possible. And between those two extremes, there's room for everything else.

But when you're dealing with a phobia —no matter what kind— you feel like you don't have a choice. You feel trapped by a restriction that keeps you from living a fulfilling life. And honestly, you can't live a fulfilling life that way, because fulfillment requires freedom, and a phobia is like a noose around your neck. But the idea that you can't choose is flat-out false, and I'm going to explain why.

YOU CHOOSE THE LIFE YOU WANT TO LIVE

I knew some people with social phobia who hid behind their condition every chance they got. They were honestly just rude people who would walk right past others and then go, "Oh, poor me, I have a phobia...!" I mean, some people are experts at hiding behind their problems —especially when you have someone enabling you, which was exactly my case. It's not that my parents were happy about me wasting my days at home, but they didn't do anything to help me break out of it either. It was a toxic mix of overprotection and pressure, with zero balance or middle ground. They were terrified that I would leave them, but at the same time, it killed them that my career wasn't going anywhere.

I believe that people who are forced to fend for themselves from an early age don't suffer from social phobia. I definitely had my struggles at the university —sometimes more than was healthy, with all the sleepless nights and hard work— but back home, I had everything I needed and even a weekly allowance. So, as harsh as it may sound, ask yourself this: Are you dealing with social phobia, or are you just spoiled? Is it our fault that we isolate ourselves, or did others isolate us? Maybe it's a mix of both, but the good news is, like I've already told you, you always have a choice.

I decided to turn my back on the world for years, until one day, I told myself that enough was enough. If you're still really young, I hope it won't take you as long as it took me to realize this: you are free, you are capable, and you are the one who decides. We have the power to change —to recognize that we've already changed in the past, even if it was for the worse. We aren't set in stone. We can move forward or backward. We can fall a thousand times and get right back up a thousand times.

I'm not telling you this just to talk, or as a therapist looking at the problem from the outside. I'm telling you this because I never stop falling and getting back up, and I don't think I ever will. The hard truth is that we are our own worst enemies. A phobia is a poison that, even after you've overcome it, keeps lying in wait.

DON'T BE YOUR OWN WORST ENEMY

I know you're reading this right now and a little voice in your head is saying, "Her case isn't like mine. What does she know? That's all well and good, but the second I close this book, I'll be completely alone with my monster again," and so on. Of course, no two cases are exactly the same, and I'm not here to tell you what to do. If your situation is "worse" than mine, I might not have the right to give you advice, but I truly hope that some of what I'm sharing will help you.

The most important piece of advice I can give you is actually pretty simple: If you want to get out of there, you can. Period. That's it. You don't need to pump yourself full of pills or have a master's degree in psychology. You just have to listen to yourself— no matter how terrified you are— and find that lever, that spark, that one thing that will propel you forward.

I know how much effort it takes, but stop and think about it: you shouldn't only focus on what it takes to change, but also on what you'll lose if you don't. You can lose everything. You can end up locked away as if you were in prison —which you're not. As if you had lost your arms and legs —which you haven't. As if you had never done a single thing right since the day you were born — which you haven't.

We set ourselves up for failure when we set our goals too high —when we want to be the most popular kid in school, the life of the party, or have a hundred friends. Have you ever thought about people who face actual, physical barriers? Some people win

Olympic medals despite missing arms or legs. I remember a documentary about a woman who was born without arms and was raising a baby all on her own. She did absolutely everything with her feet and mouth. When you hear a story like that, you realize how ridiculous your own fears can be.

I don't want to downplay the problem either. It's not just about wishful thinking or fantasy. There is something in our minds that derailed at some point. We may not be physically disabled, but in a way, we are emotionally disabled. Our emotional intelligence is underdeveloped, perhaps because our rational intelligence is overdeveloped. If, like me, you grew up surrounded by books and had barely any contact with friends, it only makes sense that you didn't build many social skills. No one ever taught me how to cultivate interpersonal relationships. On the contrary, I was encouraged to view others either as people with lesser intellectual abilities to be despised, or as gifted rivals.

During my childhood in the 1980s, holistic human development wasn't a priority in our educational system. You were just there to absorb knowledge, and that was it. Even gym class was treated as a secondary subject at my school. Art programs barely played a role either, even though they're so useful for boosting imagination and cutting down stress. Speaking of imagination, it was an absolute lifeline for me. When you grow up with next to no friends, you have to find ways to keep yourself busy. In a way, that makes you stronger —even if you don't realize it during those years of brutal loneliness. I told you before that some extroverts hide their fear of being alone, and I think they're dealing with a similar problem to ours, just in reverse. We've developed a deep aversion to social contact, while they crave it like a drug.

Speaking of drugs... The pharmaceutical industry thrives on two main sources of income: the chronically ill and the unhappy. No one in Big Pharma is interested in curing chronic illness —as harsh as that may sound. And as for the unhappy, the depressed, and the phobic? Well, they get to enjoy a whole laundry list of pills that promise quick euphoria. Once you get hooked on them —which is practically inevitable— you become pure profit for the drug companies.

Fortunately, I've never been to a psychiatrist, but I know how it goes: they give you a pat on the back and prescribe a cocktail of pills that are supposed to relax you and cheer you up. It's pathetic. A pill might mask the problem, but it doesn't cure it. In fact, it just makes things worse. The good news is that there is a solution. The bad news is that it's not as simple as swallowing a damn pill. The solution is this:

Change your mindset, and your perspective will shift.

This statement is true, even if you don't know how to put it into practice just yet. Because despite the inevitable suffering, a phobia actually has its advantages...

IS SOCIAL PHOBIA WORKING TO YOUR ADVANTAGE?

Yes, don't look away —I'm not your therapist, I know exactly where you stand. You quickly do the math and realize that you still have time to change, that you don't lack shelter or food at the moment, and that you can just be a young hikikomori until you die of old age, assuming you can afford it. But when Mom and Dad stop enabling you —or worse, when they're no longer around— you're going to get the shock of your life. Maybe only then will you have a Plan B ready: checking out early, now that nobody is left to look out for you.

I'm not going to sugarcoat things, because that's the only way I can get you to snap out of it. Yes, we're incredibly hard on ourselves — which is exactly why we are the way we are. But you know what? We actually operate on a double standard: we get completely overwhelmed by the tiniest, most irrelevant details, yet we totally neglect the absolute basics.

Of course, it's not our fault. We were raised that way, circumstances are what they are, and we are who we are. We don't have the resources or the personality of the people who think they're all that, just like they don't have parents like ours. Our parents might have been full of good intentions —after all, no one comes with a parenting manual— but they just didn't know how to handle us. Or maybe nobody in the entire world knows how to deal with a problem like this.

I was settled into my comfort zone. Just reading and watching movies was enough for me, and at least I was lucky enough to be free of everything else: obligations, unwanted relationships, appointments, routines —problems, in short. I took a snapshot of my life, and it didn't look too bad. Of course, it was all a lie, but it's like being anorexic and looking in the mirror thinking you look great.

I thought I had a family, a nest, a refuge that would always be there. But parents grow old, they die, and before that even happens, the bomb can explode: they aren't perfect either, and who's to say the parent-child relationship isn't just a vicious cycle of mutual selfishness? You took care of me as a child, so I have to take care of you when you get old. Even siblings are only around out of pure selfishness. As soon as they start their own families, they won't even reach out to you anymore —unless they want to use you as a babysitter for their kids, who will also ignore you the second they build their own lives.

And what about friends? Purely transactional, right? People mostly look for friends to tag along in activities they'd rarely do on their own. And of course, they'll let you down too, or you'll stop being a priority in their lives the second they get into a relationship.

SOCIETY IS TO BLAME

Society is structured in a way that if you step out of the cycle, you're left completely isolated. You're supposed to have friends, a partner, a family. You have to be compulsively social to keep the wheel turning, because it makes more sense financially and politically. It's way easier to manipulate a herd. Anyone who breaks away from the norm is the oddball who needs to be crushed, a threat that must be punished. Loneliness is treated like a modern-day leprosy —they literally call it the "loneliness epidemic." And ironically, it's that exact pressure to be social that ends up making us sick.

At this point, I have to confess something: I can only tolerate a handful of people. I have less and less patience for wasting my energy on people who mean nothing to me or just make me feel guilty. I've completely cut out toxic people from my life, and let me tell you, it has been incredibly liberating.

I don't want to sell you a lie. I don't want you to finish this book thinking that everyone out there is wonderful and that we're missing out on something amazing by not being part of the community on some level. No. There are some people out there who are pure scum, and honestly, people like that are probably the reason we fold our wings and retreat into our safe spaces.

I'm not trying to teach you how to be friendlier to everyone. I'm not trying to convince you to stop being introverted —that's neither better nor worse than being extroverted. You don't have to greet strangers on the street, or make small talk in the elevator or at the supermarket checkout. I don't recommend taking a job in a crowded office if the mere thought of it makes you break out in a cold sweat, either. You have every right to set your boundaries, put up a "no trespassing" sign, and retreat into your bubble whenever you need to or just feel like it.

I CLAIM MY RIGHT TO
BE AN INTROVERT

When I have a social obligation —which, fortunately, isn't very often since I was cut off from everyone for years— I need a few days to steel myself for the exhausting situation, and another few days to recover afterward. I don't like being around people. I hate being around strangers; it feels like a chore, an unpleasant experience that completely drains my energy.

The difference now is that I can handle it without being on the verge of tears. I just do it. Sometimes better, sometimes worse, sometimes with more enthusiasm, sometimes with less —but I do it... because I can. If I had the choice, I'd still much rather stay at home, but I've finally crossed the line to "I can do it."

I think the best thing you can do is work on your social phobia — not so you can force yourself into unpleasant situations that are tough even for people without a phobia, but to live a better life with the people you actually want to be around. Friends, a partner, casual acquaintances, maybe clients... Those should be your goals. It's not about overcoming a phobia just so you can tolerate the company of your annoying sister-in-law. She probably hates your guts too, and that's totally fine, because some people just don't click, period.

THE PRICE OF
STAYING THE SAME

I assume you're familiar with Charles Dickens' A Christmas Carol. It's the story of a greedy old man who gets visited by three ghosts on Christmas Eve: the Ghost of Christmas Past, the Ghost of Christmas Present, and the Ghost of Christmas Future. In the past, he was a generous, cheerful young man —until he became obsessed with money and ended up dying alone, despised by everyone. As the third spirit shows him, that is the exact fate waiting for him if he doesn't change.

For several years in a row, I made a tradition of reading this story at Christmas. I was already dealing with depression back then, and I realized I was well on my way to becoming a bitter old curmudgeon just like the main character. I comforted myself with the thought that I was still just in time to avoid dying alone, with nobody to miss me.

Changing is hard —really hard. It takes so much effort that many people don't even try, or they try and fail. Regardless of the reason, you can always try to change your life, whether it's on a whim or out of sheer necessity. Think of all the possibilities: losing weight, working out more, quitting smoking —the list goes on. If it were easy, everyone would do it. There would be no imperfect people; we'd simply snap our fingers and create a brand-new life for ourselves.

What I mean is that *everyone* has problems, and they all wish they had a magic wand to solve them. Becoming more social is a goal that could add massive value to your life —or it could literally be the thing that saves you from death. Yes, it's no exaggeration to say that extreme isolation can lead to death.

I want to recommend another book to you (both are very short, by the way): *Bartleby, the Scrivener* by Herman Melville. It's the story of an introverted man who confines himself to working in the darkest corner of his office, preferring to fly under the radar. He starts repeating a single phrase: "I would prefer not to." From that point on, he does less and less, until he merely exists —like a piece of furniture. The ending is tragic, of course; he dies with nobody there to miss him.

You can die from social phobia, just like you can die from almost anything. If you isolate yourself too much, you'll get depressed — and depression isn't just a disease of the mind, it's a disease of the body, too. I don't need to tell you how miserable it can make you feel. I actually became anemic because I didn't feel like doing any-thing, not even eating. Other people become overweight or end up taking their own lives. In short, it's an illness, and if it's not treated in time, it can spiral into something much worse and become a chronic, lifelong battle.

I know you want to break out of this cycle —that's exactly why you're reading this book. But sometimes, we need a reminder of the price we'll pay if we don't. Please, also remember that this is a battle being fought by so many people all over the world, for all kinds of reasons.

SOCIAL ANXIETY DISORDER (SAD)

Social phobia was rebranded quite a while ago. It's now called SAD: Social Anxiety Disorder. I find it kind of funny how therapists label absolutely everything as a disorder instead of just accepting that we all have different personalities. Honestly, I don't think anyone can escape getting diagnosed with a disorder these days —the list is just too long. Ultimately, it doesn't matter what you call it, but let's take a quick look at both terms.

Social phobia: That sounds like you just don't like being around people, the exact same way someone with arachnophobia hates having spiders around. I actually like this term, though I admit that SAD gives you more information about the actual problem: Social Anxiety Disorder. Disorder... To be honest, I hate being told I have a disorder. Or maybe my real issue is that I'm just in denial. The anxiety part, though? That's definitely justified. It's true —we get anxious when it comes to interacting with others. But if that's the case, then more than half the world's population has an anxiety disorder, because the potential triggers for stress are practically endless.

I'm just not a fan of putting so many labels on ourselves. Deep down, we're really not that different from everyone else. Or at least, there was a time when we were completely "normal."

No matter how far we've strayed from that point or how bad we feel right now, we can always restore that lost balance.

YOUR BEST FRIEND AND YOUR WORST ENEMY

I'm going to introduce you to "someone" who is crucial to your recovery —and, of course, to your relapses. It's the exact same thing in both cases, and it's entirely up to you whether you use it to your advantage or disadvantage.

Imagine you're sailing a sailboat (and do yourself a favor: don't overthink or roll your eyes at an example just because you think it'll never happen to you). With a sail, you're completely dependent on the wind. If the wind is blowing against you, it'll be impossible to steer the boat or even move forward. But when it's in your favor, everything runs smoothly.

In this life, it's rare for everything to be dead calm —meaning it's rare for there to be no wind at all to push you forward. In fact, a total lack of wind is a complete nightmare when you're out on a sailboat in the open ocean.

But I'll stop with the comparisons there. I'm referring to something more abstract, yet more real: inertia. Maybe you've come across this term in class before, or you already know what I'm talking about. If you're still pretty young, let me briefly explain what it means. Inertia is simply the power of habit. That's all there is to it —it's that simple.

If you wake up at the exact same time every day without an alarm, that's inertia. If you never greet your neighbors, that's also inertia. Inertia is usually an automatic response that happens without any effort, but that's not always the case. The things we do in everyday life were actually hard to learn at first: standing up, walking, tying our shoes... We didn't know how to do any of this at birth. We were a blank slate, and every single step took time.

Social dynamics are no exception. Some people seem to have a natural talent for it, and yet I'm sure they were just as nervous on their very first day of school.

By the way, if you're still in school —and I'm assuming you're going through hell right now as the antisocial oddball, or maybe you've just gone numb to it because you think it doesn't affect you anymore— you have to remember that it's just a temporary phase. I had a brutal time in school, and honestly, that's probably where this whole mess started. But back then, I didn't realize that time actually moves on, and that eventually, the blessed moment comes when it's all over for good.

But back to inertia. Inertia can be your friend or your enemy —remember that. It's not up to inertia to decide which one it is. It's up to YOU. You decide. You already have the "no." You're already living in absolute loneliness —or well on your way to it. You're stuck doing the exact same thing every day and suffering because of it. You already have all this crap. You have absolutely nothing to lose by taking a little peek into the world of possibilities you're missing out on just because you think things are a certain way, when they really aren't.

Look at how a bicycle works. At first, it's a struggle to get it moving and build up speed, but then it keeps coasting on its own until you need to pedal again. If you suddenly do something unexpected, you might even fall, depending on how much you let yourself go. Well, that's life: at first, everything is hard; then, you can coast a little; and after that, you constantly have to readjust your position and your course.

This applies to both the person with social phobia and the most popular kid in school. Life isn't easy for anyone. That's a pretty bleak consolation, but it's the only real one.

SOCIAL INERTIA

Let's take a look at how inertia and social phobia are connected.

Most people with social phobia operate the exact same way. We become shy —even if we weren't before— and things turn chronic, especially around puberty. We live our lives under a magnifying glass, trapped by perfectionism. We completely misinterpret reality, to the point where we end up feeling like we're in a totally different galaxy from everyone else.

But look at the bright side: the fact that our stories are so similar is actually a positive thing. I mean, if we all got from point A to point B following the exact same steps, without exception, then it means we can reverse the situation just by retracing those steps. Now, I'm not saying we can go back to being babies in diapers; that would be like trying to squeeze toothpaste back into the tube. Logically, it's not about traveling back in time. Even if that were possible, it wouldn't be a quick fix. Once we start isolating ourselves, our brains actually change, and you can't just hit reformat.

But it's not impossible —and that's the good news. It's been proven that our brains can still learn new things, no matter how old we get. So it's never too late to climb out of the pit of social phobia. This time, though, we're going to approach it differently: step by step.

FIRST STEP: IT'S NOT DOING YOU ANY GOOD TO BE PHOBIC

Our worst enemy lies right within ourselves. This villain is the one who brought us to where we are now, even if it wasn't their idea in the first place. It is not our fault that we lack social skills —it's the fault of the entire educational, social, and family system.

But when your inner enemy builds up momentum, the miserable bastard does it on purpose. At that point, it doesn't even need anyone else to bully it, because it makes its own life —and yours— a living hell. First, we feel isolated, and then we consciously seek out isolation. And to make matters worse, we have this little inner voice that tells us, "It's not so bad on this lonely island." Because let's face it, we can get along quite well on our own. If you don't have to go out and earn a living, you can easily pass the time with video games, TV series, or whatever else you do to keep yourself entertained.

But a day will come —maybe next year, maybe in twenty years — when keeping yourself entertained is going to get harder and harder. Not to mention that your comfy setup at home is going to vanish. Believe me, it will. You'll have to live like an adult, and if you're forced to start doing that in your thirties or forties, you're going to be a total outsider —a terrified child who sees enemies everywhere. It's just like school: you can't even imagine the day it'll finally end, for better or for worse, but everything comes and everything ends. It doesn't matter if your family is rich or poor;

you grew up lacking the absolute basics. Neither money nor your relatives will be able to save you from the fall when it hits. I'm telling you, that moment will come, and way sooner than you think.

Social phobia takes away something essential for a fulfilling life: freedom. Because let's be honest, you are not free. What else would you call it when you're unable to meet new people, try new things, or just hang out with others? Is it freedom to live locked away just because you're avoiding people? Is it freedom to let your fears run your life? You are not free, and because of that, you can never be happy.

There are endless debates about what the key to happiness is — whether it's this or that, whether you should dedicate your life to others, live in a hippie commune, or travel the world. But the absolute first step to happiness is freedom. Without it, nothing else matters. You need the freedom to choose, but with the barriers your mind builds up, happiness is only possible inside that imaginary safe space you've created for yourself.

I confess that I've always lived in my own world, and that's not necessarily a bad thing, because reality seemed pretty ugly to me. The problem is that you fall into this inertia of living half a life, and you actually convince yourself that it's great. And just like that, the years pass by. You never know what love is, you go to your grave a virgin, you miss out on everything life has to offer, and then it's simply too late to do anything about it.

MY HEALING PATH

I'll briefly summarize my life —though honestly, not much has happened. I stayed in higher education until I was in my thirties. As a teenager, around fourteen, I fell into a deep depression because I felt completely isolated from the world. Thanks to my habit of listening to music, I managed to be happy on my own for two decades. From my school days until I started working, I only had one friend. When I finally entered the workforce — under pressure from my family, not because I wanted to— my life consisted of going from home to work and back. Three years flew by like that.

My social phobia had worsened in college, but at work, it got even worse. The truth is, there were some truly nasty people at my workplace. But if you're unpleasant to someone who is already unpleasant, their ability to be nasty back to you is only going to increase.

At thirty-five, I became an orphan and started dating. Until then, I'd never had a boyfriend. By thirty-five, I was finally able to lead a decent adult life: I had a job, hung out with friends occasionally, and made casual small talk with my coworkers —even if I wasn't always thrilled about it.

It's funny because I actually ended up dating in a roundabout way. My mindset was: if I'm already forced to interact with people at work, I might as well channel that energy into my love life too. In my case, the workplace was the ultimate catalyst for change. Of course, my ideal scenario is still not having to work around people, but at least now I know I can do it without wanting to jump out the window.

I won't bore you with the details, but back then, it was an absolute nightmare. I would hide behind folders, wear headphones, go out to eat lunch by myself, turn down any invitation to hang out outside of work, and I even got into heated arguments with a co-worker I absolutely despised. I went to work exclusively to work, not to socialize. In fact, I talked more on the phone with clients than with the people in my own office. In the end, it was like I'd been forcibly sent to a socialization bootcamp —and honestly, it worked.

It wasn't easy to find a partner, and my lack of social skills definitely put me at a disadvantage. There are a lot of sketchy people on the internet, and that was my only option for meeting men. The system itself is good because it lets you move at your own pace. The problem is all the shady characters on dating sites, and since I was a complete newbie at this, it felt like I was swimming in shark-infested waters covered in fresh blood. Ultimately, it was a learning process —a brutal one.

I had to trick my own brain. For example, I never called it a "date." I absolutely hated that word because it felt like too big of a milestone for me. Instead, I'd tell myself I was just going to the movies with another human being, and things like that. Then, after the "non-date," I felt a sense of accomplishment, which balanced out my nerves.

After one step comes the next, and that's exactly how you have to approach things: step by step, pushing yourself a little further each time. There are no magic formulas. You just have to stop acting like a baby and take the steps you failed to take back then.

PHOBIC OR JUST FRIENDLESS?

Maybe you live in a tiny village and you're the only kid in the neighborhood. Maybe you'll develop a phobia because of it, maybe you won't. What I'm getting at is that some people with social phobia simply don't have any friends.

I remember checking out an online forum for people with social anxiety where they would arrange meetups. I never actually went to one, but I read the recaps. It was completely surreal. They would usually meet up in large groups, go to a club, and just sit there in total silence. They wouldn't even talk to each other. Yet, according to their posts, they felt more normal after this fake social gathering. To me, that was like trying to cure a fear of swimming by jumping headfirst off the highest diving board into a pool. I found it hard enough just to go on a single date, let alone meet up with a massive group of strangers —even if they were fellow phobics.

Deep down, a lot of people just don't have friends for whatever reason, but they don't actually suffer from social phobia. I don't think someone with real social phobia could ever bring themselves to hang out with a group of twenty people. I'm not even capable of doing that myself these days, let alone back when I was locked away at home.

PEOPLE ARE EVERYWHERE

Thanks to the internet, there's an alternative to social interaction for almost everything. You can shop from home — even if you still have to deal with the delivery guy for a split second— and you can make connections on social media that can serve as a substitute for real friendships.

But you can't always avoid human contact. It's not like a fear of spiders, which you can mostly avoid because you know they live in dark, damp places. People are always there, even when they're not physically in front of you —they're on the radio, on TV, and everywhere else.

If you're like me, you're not going to like that singer, or that YouTuber, or whoever —simply because you don't, period. Even if you've never exchanged a single word with them. But social phobia causes you to constantly have false thoughts and see other people in a distorted way. You might see them as a threat, or as people who make you feel miserable just because you find them unpleasant. Or you might think they're better —or even worse— than you, and look down on them because of it.

Obviously, we don't know how to judge someone for who they actually are. And that's because, back when we needed it most, we suffered from a brutal lack of camaraderie. Now, we react with the opposite extreme: "I don't need anyone anymore, fuck you!" And yet, it only takes a tiny bit of attention —a friendly word from a cashier, the unexpected warmth of a stranger— to completely disarm us and remind us that, naturally, we all crave human closeness.

And what about Christmas? Don't you suffer indescribably during that time of year? You suffer because you remember your childhood before the phobia, and you suffer because of those damn family obligations. No matter what you do, no matter what season it is, you always end up doing the exact same thing: suffering.

You suffer because of the company you're forced to endure, but also because of the company you don't have but wish you did — mainly, a partner. Once again, your mind is tricking you. Because let me tell you something: no romantic relationship is perfect, and you are never going to feel like you're in heaven just because you have a partner. You're simply swapping the problems of being single for the problems that come with being in a relationship. But then again, how could you possibly know that when you're stuck living on your lonely island?

People are no better or worse than you —stop making things up and don't be paranoid. Sure, some people are genuinely toxic, especially to your self-esteem, so you should absolutely keep them away. But like I said, people are everywhere. You'd better learn to tolerate them, because they're not just going to vanish.

MAKE THE MOST OF YOUR ISOLATION

Believe it or not, you are stronger than people who have never felt alone. And you know yourself better than anyone else. That's why you could be happy right here and now —you don't need anything else. Don't place the weight of your happiness on something external. That's the core foundation of Eastern philosophy, and in a way, you've already taken a step in that direction.

The problem —and the advantage— is that you're too smart. I've never met a single person with social anxiety who was stupid. Too much intelligence can play tricks on you, twist your thinking, and lead you to conclusions that others just can't see.

You need to focus on the right ideas and stop being your own worst enemy. For some reason, deep down, you think you deserve to be punished and to suffer. But suffering for no good reason is a choice you're making for yourself, so stop doing it right now.

HOW TO MANAGE SOCIAL PHOBIA

I don't know if it can be completely cured, but it can definitely be kept under control —just like a chronic illness that won't necessarily kill you. You can reduce it to a minimum and make sure it interferes with your life as little as possible. This is achieved through a combination of factors, primarily your lifestyle, by avoiding overwhelming situations. You don't have to be the center of attention at every party; you have the right to live in peace. I definitely claim my right to be left alone. Being shy is neither worse nor better than being extroverted.

If you don't set the bar too high, healing is much closer. Once you've decided on your ideal level of socialization —which, like I said, is entirely up to you— you need to work on your social skills. And how do you do that? Let's see... How do you learn to swim? By getting in the water. That's the only way. You have to want it and commit to it, and the first step is just dipping your toes in from the edge instead of jumping straight off the high dive.

You can wait until circumstances force your hand, like what happened to me, or you can start as soon as possible. Ideally, you should take it one step at a time. Use the internet to make connections —whether it's through chat rooms, forums, groups, or communities centered around your hobbies.

These days, there are a thousand ways to get out of your cave without ever setting foot on the street. I seriously wish I'd had the internet when I was younger. But be careful: it's just a means to an end, not the end itself. Let me explain that in more detail.

THE CYBER WORLD

The fact that you're even reading this book is thanks to the cyber world. The possibilities of the internet are limitless. Honestly, without the internet, I'd probably still be sitting in my room talking to blue unicorns. It was my lifeline in every sense: for work, for socializing, and for my love life. But it also caught me at an age when I was already making my own decisions, and I'm sure it would have done me way more harm than good as a teenager. I would have gotten bent out of shape over every single comment, spent hours stalking people on social media, and all that.

And yet, the internet still hurt me —or rather, I hurt myself, because I didn't know how to handle it. Ultimately, it's just another form of socialization that we are in no way prepared for. The problem with the internet when it comes to relationships is that you can easily blur the lines between fantasy and reality, and that's how I ran into some major roadblocks. I'd imagine I was in a romantic relationship, when to the other person, it was just a way to kill time in a chat room. I started believing people were exactly how I imagined them behind my screen. I acted like a character, even though, ironically, I was being more authentic than I ever was in real life.

So be careful not to play a character, and don't get wrapped up in other people's characters either. Use it as the positive tool it can be, and don't let it go past that. If you feel like you're getting too comfortable only talking to someone via chat, you need to break this inertia and let the connection cool down. It's hard, but if you don't put a stop to it, you could end up doing yourself some serious damage. Our ultimate goal is to meet real people in the real world

—and to do that, we obviously have to step outside.

TAKING STEPS
IN REAL LIFE

Our first step won't be to approach people directly or wait around to meet someone before going out. You need to start going to physical places, all by yourself. Start with spots where it's completely normal for people to go alone: running errands, grocery shopping during the workday when it's less crowded, going to the post office, or simply walking down one street and coming back up another. You can wear sunglasses if it helps, choose less busy streets, and all that. This simple habit will help you build up your confidence until you feel ready to venture out into busier settings that still allow you to be alone: art exhibitions, the movies, the theater, conferences, and so on.

If you feel uncomfortable while waiting in line for these activities, you can always seek refuge in your phone —though you probably already know that trick all too well. However, I recommend using it a bit differently: try writing down your impressions, or texting yourself about how you're doing and how you feel.

These are small steps that will help you make progress and feel more comfortable out in the world. And always have a Plan B in mind. Don't feel like a failure if you suddenly want to run back home, or if you end up absolutely hating the activity. Remember that even extroverts have their bad days, and that going out isn't always all it's cracked up to be.

SAY IT OR HIDE IT?

Remember: you are not your phobia. You don't have to introduce yourself by saying, "My name is X, and I have social anxiety." If you don't bring it up, it won't become the center of attention. But you can't pretend it's not there either. So you can say it, just don't make a big deal out of it. You could say things like, "I'm not a fan of large groups," "I'm just really shy," or "I find it a bit tough to meet new people," and all that.

Opening up about these things doesn't mean you feel inferior. They are simply facts, realities —and it's your way of setting boundaries so you don't end up feeling uncomfortable.

When it comes to meeting new people, it's best to find a middle ground. Another person with social anxiety will definitely understand you better, but you won't be able to help each other much —and that's just the sad reality. On the other hand, a great friend could be someone who is shy but doesn't completely freeze up and can still take part in social activities. Someone who is just a little braver than you is the perfect companion.

Naturally, it'll be tough to get along with ultra-extroverts, because they won't understand your need for isolation, and you won't be able to keep up with them anyway. The exact same thing goes for a partner. Someone who prefers low-key plans away from the crowds, who doesn't compulsively seek out friends, and who doesn't expect you to go to a party every single week will fit right in with your lifestyle.

TAKE GOOD CARE OF YOURSELF, IN THE TRUEST SENSE OF THE WORD

We are perfectionists, and our social anxiety is deeply rooted in that. We worry that we can't keep up with others, we're terrified of being watched and judged, and the real issue is that we are our own harshest critics. Allow yourself to fail, to make mistakes, and to do things even if they're not perfect. Stop overthinking and just pick an activity you actually enjoy.

Use humor —it helps with absolutely everything. Get moving, even if it's just in your own room or a quick ten-minute walk. The goal is to start feeling good within a minute. Once you get some practice, it won't take any extra time at all.

You don't need pills for this. You just need to boost your well-being by shutting down your negative thoughts and doing things that actually make you feel good. Listen to music, take a hot shower, watch your favorite comedy, paint, sing —in short, do whatever you know will lift your spirits.

You might think I'm straying from the topic, or that none of this has anything to do with overcoming social phobia. But the truth is, the problem is entirely in your head. Because of that, the only way out is to become a healthier person —both mentally and physically.

When you feel better, you'll be stronger and better equipped to deal with this and many other problems. Eventually, you'll even be able to decide whether you want to remain a misanthrope for the rest of your life.

In any case, don't be afraid to try and manage your phobia. Be less hard on yourself, and you'll be less hard on the rest of humanity. You'll be happier, and you won't give anyone the power to dictate your self-esteem.

I hope that at least one simple paragraph in this book proves useful to you. It could be the first step toward the rest of your life — and that's the most important thing when we embark on a journey. The beginning is what truly counts.

I hope you recover soon from this poison that is social phobia. I am absolutely sure that you are worth a lot and that you can achieve anything you set your mind to. Don't let anyone convince you otherwise —starting with your own mind.

I wish you all the best.